**Didier Janicot**
Sixth Dan / Sports Instructor
Dir., French School of Judo-Jujitsu

**Gilbert Pouillart**
Prof., P. E. / Judo Instructor
Doctor of Sociology

# *Judo* Techniques and Tactics

In cooperation with Christophe Gagliano
Preface by Jean-Luc Rougé
Illustrations by Richard Roussel

**Sterling Publishing Co., Inc.**
New York

## PHOTO CREDITS

**D. Chauvet (Milan):** Pages 1, 3, 5, 10, 14, 15, 16, 17, 18, 20, 22, 23 (top), 24, 25, 26, 27, 28, 30, 31 32, 33, 35, 36, 38, 39, 40, 41, 42, 43, 44, 45 (except bottom), 47, 49, 51 (top), 53, 54, 55, 56, 58, 59, 60, 61, 64, 65, 66, 67, 68, 69, 70, 72, 74, 78, 79, 80, 81 (except bottom), 82, 83, 84, 85, 86, 87, 89.

**Tempsports:** Pages 2-3, 3, 6, 8 (middle, bottom), 12, 23 (bottom), 29, 45 (bottom), 48, 51 (bottom), 52, 62, 71, 75, 77, 81, (bottom), 88, 90, 92, 94, 95, 96, 97, 98.

Translated by Yana Melnikova
Edited by Claire Bazinet

**Library of Congress Cataloging-in-Publication Data**
Janicot, Didier
    [Judo. English]
    Judo: techniques and tactics / Didier Janicot, Gilbert Pouillart;
in cooperation with Christophe Gagliano; preface by Jean-Luc Rougé;
illustrations by Richard Roussel; translated by Yana Melnikova].
       p. cm.
    Includes index.
    ISBN 0-8069-1970-1
       1. Judo. I. Pouillart, Gilbert. II. Gagliano, Christophe. III. Title.
    GV1114.J37  2000
    796.815'2—dc21

                   99-056152
10  9  8  7  6  5  4  3  2  1

Published by Sterling Publishing Company, Inc.
387 Park Avenue South, New York, N.Y. 10016
First published by Editions MILAN, 300 rue Léon-Joulin,
31101 Toulouse Cedex 01 France
© 1997 by Editions MILAN
English translation © 2000 by Sterling Publishing Co., Inc.
Distributed in Canada by Sterling Publishing
C/o Canadian Manda Group, One Atlantic Avenue, Suite 105,
Toronto, Ontario, Canada M6K 3E7
Distributed in Great Britain and Europe by Chris Lloyd,
463 Ashley Road, Parkstone, Poole, Dorset, BH14 0AX, England
Distributed in Australia by Capricorn Link (Australia) Pty Ltd.
P.O. Box 6651, Baulkham Hills, Business Centre, NSW 2153, Australia
*Printed in China*
*All rights reserved*

Sterling  ISBN 0-8069-1970-1

*J*udo is a school for living, with grade levels and dans that allow you, step by step, to measure your progress through the three elements of judo-jujitsu: shin, ghi and tai. The goal of judo instructors is not only to train champions and masters of technique in a martial art, but to help their students to feel good about themselves and their lives, to exist in harmony with their surroundings, and to be good citizens.

Prepared in close cooperation with the judo-jujitsu school of the French Federation of Judo, the authors Didier Janicot, director of the school, and Gilbert Pouillart have, in this book, addressed simply and precisely the many concerns and questions judo students have about the training.

The road to becoming a shihan (a role model) is a long one This book will guide you in taking the proper direction so that later, you alone, based on what you have learned, can follow your own way. Judo (the path of flexibility) is not an exercise, but a mode of self-expression.

*Jean-Luc Rougé*
Director, French Federation of Judo, Jujitsu,
Kendo and Associated Diciplines (F.F.J.D.A.)
1975 World Champion

# Contents

**We, the *Judoka*,** gratefully remember Dr. Jigoro Kano (1860–1938), who in Japan formulated and developed judo. Through it he expressed the mottoes "maximum efficiency, minimal effort" and also "mutual prosperity and kind deeds"…which still apply. In the form of sport and martial art, judo remains today a means of spiritual and physical improvement, of friendship and of cooperation in relation to others.

**General**
**Improvement 37**

## Personal Improvement 63

## Competition 91

*Ryoko Tamura, Japan, born in 1975*

A star in her own country, she keeps up the Japanese tradition of judo on tatami mats all over the world. World champion many times, she also twice made the Olympic finals.

# Judo

**martial art / sport / school of life / passion**

You are about to enter the world of judo, a discovery that will bring into your life many emotions—mostly pleasure and joy. You will make numerous friends who will help you improve, becoming more precise, skillful, supple, and stronger. A wonderful and exciting adventure is about to open before you. Let's be on our way!

# What Is Judo?

*Judo is, first of all:*

◆ An activity that can be practiced in different ways to bring pleasure to the young and the less young, to boys and to girls, and to champions and novices alike.

◆ A big family: the judoka are happy to meet each other on the mats...and often in daily life.

◆ Training and education that allows you to improve both physically and mentally. You become stronger, faster, more flexible and more agile. Judo helps you increase your self-control, as well as your ability to make decisions and to persevere in the face of difficulty or fatigue.

*Judo is also:*

◆ A great international sport: an Olympic sport that gathers thousands of players and organizers of prestigious competitions. International championships are held in various countries throughout the world so that hundreds of thousands of judoka from cities and towns and villages can compete—and conquering champions win and are proud to have earned the most desirable medals.

*Judo is, above all:*

◆ A martial art: you can always find in it a chance and the means to develop your own personality, together with friends and with their help. Being a judoka could become your lifestyle.

*This book was written to:*

◆ Help you understand judo better, its rules, techniques and tactical ideas for organized combat, and the programs for all belts through to the first *dan* black belt.

◆ Help you study judo: you really learn on a tatami but in order to understand judo, you also have to think about it when you are not on the mats.

◆ Encourage you to work seriously and with pleasure. Enjoyment from doing judo is not only the prerogative of great champions; all judoka can know and preserve it.

No book can replace a personal instructor, one who knows you well and is with you on the mat to constantly help improve technique. But at home, when it's not the day or time for judo, this book is a friend to take up gladly—to "think" judo, examine details, and better understand how and what you do.

# *Memorize well these little icons and their meanings.*

*These images are used throughout the book to help you to better focus on the specific aspect of judo being taken up in the various paragraphs.*

### Shin
The mind, inner state, spiritual qualities: such as modesty, courage, loyalty, concentration, fairness and kindness

### Ghi
Basic knowledge: techniques and tactics

### Tai
The body: the physical qualities, combat efficiency

### Nagewaza
Standing techniques: throws

### Transition
The standing/ground link

### Referee
Rules and terms

### Newaza
Ground techniques: holds, locks and chokes

# Your First Steps

## the opening door

*In judo, as in life's other activities, the beginning is fundamental. A good start helps ensure progress. Even if you have already been practicing judo, read and pay close attention to this chapter.*

# The Dojo

*Wherever you live, you will probably be able to find near your home a club dedicated to the martial arts and a* dojo *where you can study and practice judo.*

You can start studying judo at the age of 6, but it is possible to begin at any age.

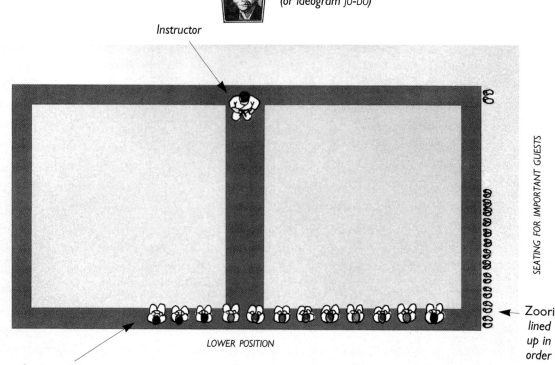

PLACE OF HONOR

*Portrait of Dr. Kano (or ideogram JU-DO)*

*Instructor*

SEATING FOR OCCASIONAL VISITORS

SEATING FOR IMPORTANT GUESTS

Zoori lined up in order

LOWER POSITION

*Students, belts arranged in ascending order. (Eldest in the highest grade announces "Rei"—bow.)*

# Dressing for Judo

Judo fighters wear a white outfit, or *judogi*, consisting of trousers, a jacket without fastenings and a belt. The purpose of the *judogi* is not to make you "look good" or show that you practice judo. For opponents, it is a convenient fighting tool. Wearing *judoji* allows you to grab someone, try to bring him where you want, make him fall, keep him on his back…all without harming him.

The outfit is completed by the *zoori*, the "slippers" that you use to walk around the dojo when you are not on the *tatami*: such as the locker rooms, the halls and in restrooms. You slip them on when you leave the mat to avoid catching cold and to keep your feet clean. Remember, not only do your feet touch the *tatami*, but your body and sometimes your face are pressed against it.

## How to dress for judo

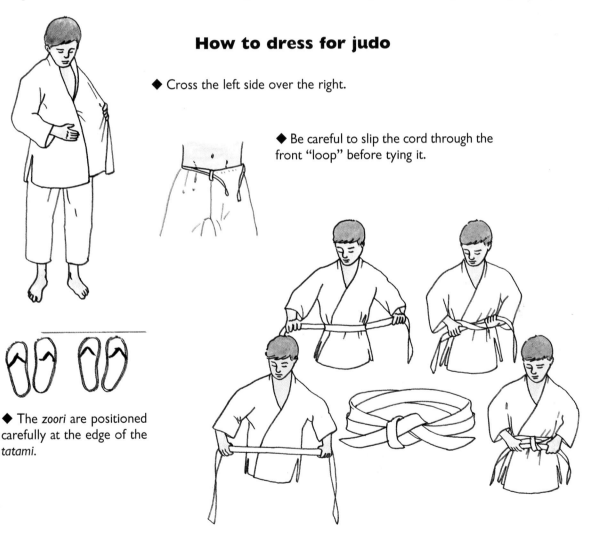

◆ Cross the left side over the right.

◆ Be careful to slip the cord through the front "loop" before tying it.

◆ The *zoori* are positioned carefully at the edge of the *tatami*.

◆ The *obi* goes around twice. It is a tied in a "square knot" (the two ends form a "mustache" before falling down).

## To do judo, you must:

◆ Wear your full *judogi*, keeping it always clean and in good condition.

◆ Cut your fingernails and toenails short so they are not bent painfully backward or accidentally scratch your partner.

◆ Remove from your person everything that might cause an injury: especially jewelry. (If you wear glasses or retainers, ask your instructor what he or she wants you to do.)

## From white to black belt

As a beginner, you start off as a white belt, no matter your age; but there is a minimum age for passing to the next grade, that is, to the new belt.

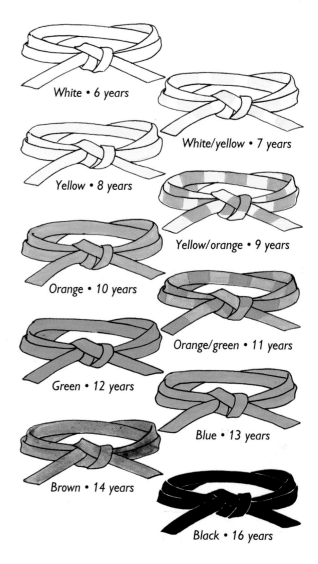

White • 6 years

White/yellow • 7 years

Yellow • 8 years

Yellow/orange • 9 years

Orange • 10 years

Orange/green • 11 years

Green • 12 years

Blue • 13 years

Brown • 14 years

Black • 16 years

*This book will accompany you along the way to the first grade of the black belt (shodan), because one day you will be a black belt...as long as you keep studying and training.*

**The International Judo Federation (I.J.F.) is composed of five continental unions (Europe, Asia, Oceania, Pan-America, and Africa) and brings together more than 175 countries.**

# *Judo Mat: The Tatami*

You will soon realize that the *tatami*, the judo mat, is great for allowing you to move quickly and easily in any position—standing, on all fours or lying down. It is not soft, so you won't twist an ankle; but at the same time it is not hard, so you don't hurt yourself when falling.

The 2 by 1 meter "individual" mats are laid together, side by side, as needed for practice space.

# *Falls (Ukemiwaza)*

*Falling is a part of judo: combat always starts while standing, and you win by throwing your opponent on his back. Therefore, from the beginning you must learn to fall without hurting yourself and learn to throw an opponent without harming him.*

**When falling onto the *tatami*, you need to roll like a giant ball whether you fall**...

◆ *backward*

◆ *on your side*

◆ *or forward*

Your back must always be kept rounded, like a turtle's shell.

When you want to throw your partner, keep hold of his sleeve and move it toward the *tatami*. Be careful to keep your balance so that you don't fall on top of him.

If you do what your instructor tells you, you won't be afraid of falling. Instead, taking falls will become your pleasure and pride. A good judo throw requires one partner who can throw well and another who can land well.

**Remember these important points:**
- Your head never touches the *tatami*; it's "hidden in the shell."
- Your legs remain apart (do not keep your knees together).
- Only your back and feet come into contact with the *tatami*. Your ankles, knees and shoulders should not hit the mat. Above all, don't fall on your arms.

# The Slap

*It's the end of the fall. The whole arm, from the back of the shoulder to the palm of the hand, strikes the tatami at the same time—very strongly. This is a very short action; the hand lifts off the ground right after the slap.*

◆ When you fall backwards, you strike with both arms.

◆ During a lateral or forward fall, you strike with the arm closest to the ground.

Learn to slap the mat on landing right from the start: make it a point of reminding yourself to do it every time. Later, when you are thrown harder and faster, the slap will help you to cushion your fall and get up immediately.

# *Your First Class*

One feels a little overwhelmed, but also eager to be on the *tatami*.

GRAND (STANDING)
BOW, AT THE START

### How does this happen?

◆ Come to the *dojo* early, to be ready before the start of class;

◆ In the locker room, put your *judogi* on, tie your belt (with the help of older classmates or, often, the instructor);

◆ Slip on your *zoori*, decide if you need to use the bathroom (once you're on the *tatami*, you won't leave it until the end of class);

◆ Place your *zoori* carefully at the edge of the *tatami* and bow, as in Japanese tradition, by leaning forward from a standing position.

◆ Stand, together with your classmates, for the "grand starting bow."

GRAND (KNEELING)
BOW, AT THE END

At the end of the class, when, after *zarei* (ceremonial kneeling bow which concludes the session), you leave the mats, you will have learned many things:

◆ In judo you fight but do not clash violently: you are trying to win, but without hurting anybody. This is a rule of judo: Never harm anyone.

◆ In judo, you do not start an exercise or combat without bowing to your partner and you do not leave without bowing to him again.

◆ On the *tatami* you have only friends: first the instructor, who only wants to help you learn better and faster, then the opponents, who will become your teammates. You will know them all by their first names, do judo with them, study along with them and with their help. You can't practice judo alone!

Now you have only to take a shower, pack your bag, return home, and wait eagerly for the next class.

# The Referee

*Judo has, as you will learn, its own rules and specific vocabulary. At the back of this book is a complete glossary, but we want to familiarize you here with a few basic words and signals of the referee.*

**Hajime:** begin. Before the referee signals the start of combat, the two fighters stand at a distance facing each other.

**Matte:** halt. Both fighters immediately stop, release each other and return to their original starting positions.

**Ippon:** end of fight. There is a winner

**Osaekomi:** hold. Announced at start of a hold-down.

**Toketa:** hold broken. Announced when a player escapes from a hold-down.

# Beginning Judo

## finding home and family

After the first class there is another one…then another one…and little by little, step by step as you progress, you find your place in the great judo family. Respect for the rules and for the opponent, understanding the symbols and learning the judo techniques will become second nature.

# *Part of a Family*

**To be a good *judoka*, you must:**

◆ Always be on time.

◆ Be in a good mood (it's easy when doing something you enjoy with an instructor and friends that you like).

◆ Never forget a single bow; it's a way to show that you are a combatant, not an aggressor, and that you are thankful to your partner opponents, who are helping you to improve.

◆ Respect the golden rules of judo:

● Grab only by the cloth.

● Never strike a partner, avoid twisting or turning of the joints or squeezing the neck.

● Avoid hitting the walls and leaving the *tatami*.

● Let go and step back once an opponent submits. This is signaled by tapping the *tatami* or his body a few times with a free hand or leg.

*J*udo does not tolerate brutality: it is the sport of clever people. You bring the other where you want, despite his will and often without him even noticing! That is what good judo is about.

All young *judoka* smile during *randori* (training fights): it's an exciting, spirited game, with everybody trying to display superior speed and skill.

**To play well, you must know the rules, apply those rules based on the golden rule, and respect the referee's decisions.**

**What do you have to do to win?**

◆ Make your partner fall on his back          or

◆ Keep your partner lying on his back on the mat for the specified amount of time.

If one of these actions is accomplished, you obtain an *ippon*.
But to win, you have to learn *how* to be awarded an *ippon*.

# Techniques and Tactics

*The movements performed by athletes are what allow you to recognize and identify a sport. It is those moves that make up technique. In judo, the moves are extensive and varied.*

While in some sports you continually repeat a gesture—trying to perfect it—in judo, the movements change endlessly.

There are many ways to throw or hold your partner, who also may react in a great many ways. The choice of a right movement at a certain moment of the fight determines its outcome. The right tactics involve assessing a situation quickly and correctly, and working out a way to turn it into a victory. Basic judo tactics also involve using your partner's strength. Instead of trying to prevent your partner from carrying out an action, let him act…and use it to your advantage. Judo is a very subtle game that calls upon your intelligence.

We will discover here and perfect starting techniques on the basis of the situations that come up often in a fight. You will learn to recognize and use them. There is a basic principle applied in each of these "study situations." The same situation is repeated several times in a row during practice.

The partner whose role is to move in a given way is called "*uke*," and the one who tries to take advantage of the move to win is "*tori*." Naturally, everybody in turn becomes *uke* or *tori*.

# *Standing Combat : Nagewaza*

## BASIC TECHNIQUES

### 1. *Uke* retreats and pulls

**Tori seizes uke and throws him on his back:**

◆ Let *uke* pull you without resisting, then seize him—it's easy (you can move forward faster than backward)…

◆ …by moving forward in this way you will push up against him, while he is still pulling…

◆ …and place your leg behind his (*osoto-oto-shi*), to knock him backward. You can do this whenever *uke*'s legs are placed close together.

### You have several techniques to cause your partner to fall:

*Ko-uchigari*

*O-uchigari*

◆ If *uke*'s legs are positioned farther apart, it's easier to seize him "head-on" and attack his nearest leg from the inside (*ko-uchigari* or *o-uchigari*).

## 2. *Uke* advances and pushes

**Tori shifts or makes a semicircle and throws *uke* forward.** You have to learn to "leave your path." You help him advance and put an obstacle before him to make him stumble.

### There are two ways to do this:

◆ Make him trip over a low obstacle that obstructs a leg while you continue pulling on his sleeve: this way you are standing next to him and can continue to watch him.

*Sasae-tsurikomi-ashi*

*Hizaguruma*

◆ Or place a higher barrier in front of him, around which his body will pivot: you will then have turned your back to him and cannot see him.

*Note: The obstacle, or barrier, is always on the same side as the sleeve held, and you must continue holding on to your opponents by that sleeve as they fall.*

*Taiotoshi*

*Morote with block. Notice that tori's elbow is against uke's chest.*

# 3. *Uke* goes around *tori*

**Advancing toward the side on which a sleeve is held:**

◆ The easiest method would be to act as if your partner was moving forward. Once again you have to "leave your path" to make him trip over an obstacle or fall over a barrier: *ashiguruma*.

Three situations to study:

   Uke pulls and moves back
   Uke pushes and moves forward
   Uke goes around tori

Like rehearsing scenes for a martial-arts movie, you need to repeat your moves in these situations numerous times in order to learn to do them well.

*Ashiguruma*

# *Basic Tactical Concepts*

During study sessions, the only tactical concept is "I let my partner move around and can benefit by making him fall." In combat, it's a bit more complicated: there's no designated *uke*...and everyone certainly wants to be the *tori* to win. So how do you know where you are?

**Let's examine some simple scenarios:**
You were able to take the initiative because your opponent had moved back or forward, or turned in a good direction for you. You notice it right away and try a technique.

## 1. Your opponent attacks

You have to avoid the attack and take the initiative again. The basic idea: allow your opponent to act...but "in an empty space."

*He attacks by using hizaguruma.*

*You dodge, leaving him standing in an empty space.*

*You can, in turn, attack by hizaguruma.*

## 2. You attack, he dodges

Before he can take advantage and counter, if you are alert and fast, you can attack again and thus keep the initiative.

## 3. You attack, he falls

He's not completely on his back, however, so you don't score an *ippon*. You need to continue attacking him on the ground. To do this:

◆ First, don't let go of him. Then, quickly, descend to his side in order to put him on his back and hold him there with *kuzure-gesa-gatame*.

# *Ground Combat : Newaza*
# BASIC TECHNIQUES

> **The goal is to immobilize the opponent:** *osaekomi* (hold-down).
> For this call, *uke*'s back must be against the mat with *tori* on top holding him, facing away from *uke*'s legs and applying an immobilization technique. Required time of immobilization is 30 seconds.

## 1. Hold partner down on back (*osaekomi*)

**In *osaekomi*, you (or your opponent) are confronted with 4 main tactical problems:**

*Kuzure-gesa-gatame*

You will soon realize that, in order to win, you have four ways to position yourself in relation to your opponent:

◆ Next to him, sitting against his body (not on it!) while pulling on the sleeve you continue to hold. Your other hand has released his lapel and slipped under his arm, flat on the mat ◀ (*kuzure-gesa-gatame*). (This is the easiest *osaekomi* position to take when you have applied *osoto-otoshi*.)

◆ Again at his side, but lying "across" (*yoko-shiho-gatame*) ▶

◆ Behind his head, well flattened on the mat (*kami-shiho-gatame*) ▼

◆ Across his body, as flat as you can make yourself (*tate-shiho-gatame*) ▼

These four positions can get you the *ippon* you want.

# 2. Put partner on back and apply *osaekomi*

You don't always have an opportunity to apply *osaekomi* the moment your opponent is on the ground. He will do everything he can do *not* to stay on his back, *not* to be beaten. So, you will now study how to *put him* on his back, starting your maneuver while he is on his knees.

◆ You want a way to put him into position on his back.

◆ If your opponent pushes to try to knock you down, you can, as in standing combat, "get out of his path."

Often, during ground combat, your opponent will get down on all fours in order to defend himself. Once he is set in that position, you need to turn him over. There are many ways of doing this. The photographs below show some simple solutions. Right after you do it, put him in *osaekomi*.

# Basic Tactical Concepts

## 1. Your partner attacks

◆ If you're on your back, you have to position yourself in front of him quickly to catch him at once with both your arms and legs.

◆ If you can interpose one of your legs between yourself and him in one of several ways (shin across his stomach, one or two legs on his groin, "one leg inside, one leg outside"), you'll pull him against yourself. This enables you to use your leg or legs as a lever.

◆ As soon as you have carried out this maneuver, you will knock him over, regain the upper position by turning him on his back, then going into *osaekomi*.

◆ If you are on your hands and knees, he will want to turn you over. You will counter-attack by using his attack to turn him over, and move into *osaekomi*.

There are also a great number of techniques to attack from a lower position.

# 2. Your partner holds you in *osaekomi*

Don't struggle just any way. You have only a short time to free your-self. To do this, remember these three things:

◆ If you can get him on top of you (no longer "next" to you), roll over on yourself like a tree trunk down a slope, pulling him along.

He is no longer "on" you, you are no longer on your back = *toketa*.

◆ If you can take one of his feet in a "lock" (*sankaku*), you can easily turn him over.

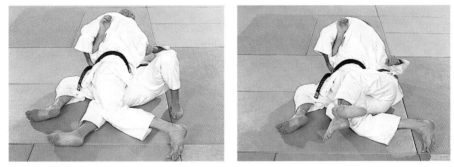

You are holding him with your feet = *toketa*.
He is not on top anymore, but next to you or beneath you = *toketa*.

◆ If he's not pressed strongly against you, you can free yourself by rolling and not pulling him along.

You are no longer on your back, your stomach is on the *tatami* = *toketa*.

# Basic Information on Direction

**The o and ko difference concerns tori :**

**o**   when tori's attacking foot crosses behind his supporting foot from behind (long course)

**ko**   when his attacking foot crosses in front of his supporting foot (short course)

KO

O

Tori's feet

**The difference between *soto* and *uchi* has to do with *uke*:**

SOTO   UCHI   UCHI   SOTO

**soto**   when *uke*'s leg is attacked from the outside

**uchi**   when *uke*'s leg is attacked from the inside

Uke's feet

MIGI   HIDARI

MAE   USHIRO

**migi**
means
"right, to
the right"

**hidari**
means
"left, to
the left"

**ma, mae**
these mean
"forward,
straight on"

**ushiro**
means
"backward,
behind"

**yoko**
means "on the side, sideways"

One year, two years of judo can pass very fast, but you will have had many classes and learned many things. At this point you already feel yourself at home on the *tatami*, you have become stronger, more skillful. You like going to meet your instructor and your friends, and being part of the judo family, whose roots reach back many years to the first of the masters, Dr. Jigoro Kano. Your progress will continue and you will gradually discover, little by little, all of the roads that make up the world of judo…and with increasing great joy!

Dr. Jigoro Kano
(1860–1938)

# General Improvement

**deeper into the "world of judo"**

*N*ow you have gone far enough into judo to be curious and to want to explore it in greater depth. You know the ceremonies well, you respect them, and you are capable of seeing them differently. You will also start to see judo combat more and more as an "exchange."

# What Does the Bow Represent?

◆ *the habit of politeness*

◆ *the regaining of one's composure, immediately after the excitement of a fight*

◆ *a way to show respect for others, as they also respect you*

◆ *a signal by which both opponents agree to scrupulously follow the rules of combat*

# What Does the Combat Represent?

◆ *something like a discussion, where each person tries to get an idea across to the other; each person not only speaks, but listens*

◆ *a way of learning more and more ways to attack...and to avoid attack; you even learn to recognize that sometimes you can use your opponent's attack to win*

# GENERAL IMPROVEMENT

## PHASE ONE

### *Yellow/Orange and Orange Belts*
# *Techniques and Tactics*

## *Standing Combat: Nagewaza*

*It's not sufficient anymore just to make someone fall: you need to actually "throw." This means that* uke *is airborne for a short moment, not touching the* tatami, *before landing there on his back.*

You have arrived at the point when your attacks are becoming more and more precise, impressive and powerful. Your throws now happen during gradually more complicated combat situations. You attack now not only when your opponent pulls you with him while shifting, but also to make him shift, or to resist his shifting, or even to provoke him to resist a fake shifting movement.

Practicing some new study situations will help you increase the number of options you have for attacking. We will provide some examples here, and you will progressively learn many technical responses to each situation studied.

**40** The principle of throwing uke in the direction of his action is always applicable, so long as his action consists of resisting yours. "*Tori* pulls, *uke* resists" is almost the same as "*uke* pulls." So, the attacks examined in the previous chapter still work, and you can add an *osotogari* to them (cutting *uke*'s leg out from under him from the outside).

*Osotogari*

## 1. *Uke* moves toward lapel *tori* holds

Here is a chance to discover a new group of techniques, the sweeps. The sweeps use the basic judo idea to perfection: "minimum effort, maximum efficiency."

*Okuri-ashi-barai* (ankle sweep). You can sweep dust, which is not heavy or stuck to the ground, but you cannot "sweep" something like a chest of drawers filled with clothing. You have to "hunt" *uke*'s leg in its movement, when it is not loaded down with the weight of his body.

## 2. *Tori* moves *uke* in circle

You "take center" and make your partner turn around you. For example, if you turn him in the direction of the lapel you hold, you can use *o-uchigari* (a technique you already know), but this time in the form of a sweep.

His leg, pushed by yours, goes farther than he expects...

*O-uchigari*

## 3. Both move to side, toward held sleeve

You can apply *ko-uchigari*, always in the form of a sweep.

*Ko-uchigari*

## 4. *Tori* pulls and steps back, *uke* follows

*Ogoshi*

Here is another study situation: your opponent, even if for only for a step or two, does not take the initiative or oppose you. You glide below him (look at the levels of the two belts) and, in turning your back to him, turn him over your hip. You must act very fast, before he can react. These are the moves to make in order to take advantage of his temporary "goodwill."

*Ippon-seoinage*

*Morote-seoinage*

These techniques, where you fling your partner over your hips or shoulder, with your back turned, feet slightly apart and knees well bent, require a lot of work. It's important to start feeling at ease in this position and to assume it as soon as an opportunity presents itself.

*Eri-seoinage*

There is another important group of techniques, which use the back. For *haraigoshi,* the first example you will learn, you "sweep" behind your partner's two legs…this means you rest on only one foot.

It seems that, for that brief moment, the weight of your two bodies rests on only a single foot. It is an overwhelming thought at first, but many study situations will show you that this throw is possible.

*Haraigoshi*

## 5. Take initiative (or keep it) after sidestep

You need to learn to fight, as much as you are able, "continually," not using separate actions with intervals where nothing much happens.

Here are two examples:

◆ The opponent attacks, you sidestep…and launch an offensive right away. It is a counter-attack. In these photos you see *uke* attacking with *o-uchigari*, *tori* sidestepping and then counter-attacking with *taiotoshi*.

◆ You attack, your opponent dodges, but also gives you a chance to make a second attack, and you go on. These photographs show two examples:

• two attacks linked back to back

*O-uchigari*

*Sidestep*

*Osotogari*

# • forward attack after rear attack is avoided

*Ko-uchigari*

*Sidestep*

*Taiotoshi*

The principle is always the same, it's the basis of judo: To win, use the actions of your opponent against him instead of exhausting yourself by attempting to prevent them.

You have already learned many throws. This does not mean that you master them all, but you can choose those you prefer to use as your best weapons in a fight. Also, knowing all of them a little helps to avoid them when they are used against you.

You have changed since you started doing judo. You have grown, becoming bigger and stronger. This will continue, and your tastes will also be changing. It is possible that, in the future, you will prefer attacks that you do not care for and don't use now. To know many attacks gives you the freedom to choose which to use when.

# *It's important to practice your favorite attacks in different directions.*

*Here are the three directions of attack:*

**forward**

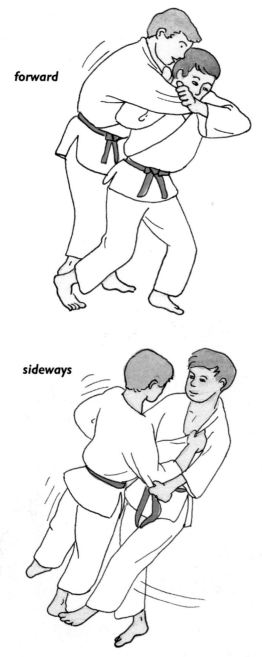

**backward**

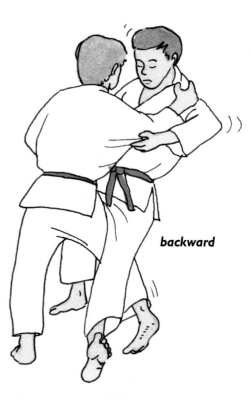

**sideways**

*If you make it a practice to "cover" all the directions of attack, you will be able to take the initiative in combat, no matter what your opponent might do. Furthermore, you could surprise him, fool him by pretending that you are attacking in one direction, when you are actually mounting an attack in a different direction.*

# Standing/Ground Link

Your opponent fell, after your attack or while trying a throw, but there's no *ippon*. You know, in this case, how to link directly to *osaekomi*, as with *kesa-gatame*. But if, to avoid the take-down, he rapidly turns and tries to lie on his stomach, you can control and turn him onto his back. Let go his lapel, then circle his arm with yours and grip your own lapel.

There are other forms of fighting from "standing/ take-down" position, more ways of following up groundwise, and other "scenarios" to start attacks, for defense and counter-attacks.

# Ground Combat : Newaza

You now know the four basic *osaekomi* positions. Soon, you will perform them with more skill and precision, and discover *kuzure* (variations useful in many different combat situations).

Above all, you will learn to link *osaekomi* without losing control of *uke*. It is less exhausting than trying to resist "in place" your opponent's attempts to free himself.

*Kuzure-gesa-gatame*

*Yoko-shiho-gatame*

You also learn to attack and win in situations where you don't have the upper hand or in those situations where your opponent has a strong defensive position.

# Training Methods

*The types of exercise the instructor makes you do are increased.*

You know a number of "study situation" exercises, used to learn or practice a technique. You have practiced *randori*, combat that goes on to the end of a set time period regardless of the number of points the fighters receive. You have taken part in refereed fights, which end when one of the opponents earns an *ippon*.

## Now here are some other ways to practice:

**Kakari-geiko:** During a set time period, a fighter is designated as either attacker or defender.

**Yaku-soku-geiko:** You are either an attacker or a defender, but in both cases your mind should be set on attacking, not defense.

**Uchikomi:** *Tori* repeats the same attack in series in order to get used to destabilizing his partner using fast, skilled movement, but without throws.

**Nagekomi:** *Tori* throws one or more opponents in a row, as fast and as strongly as possible.

Finally, you have the chance to confront for the first time *judokas* from other clubs, and make new judo friends whom you haven't even met yet. You get to know other *dojos,* other instructors. It's an opportunity to view other forms of combat and to take an accounting of your own weak and strong points.

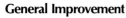

# *Refereeing*

*The rules of refereeing are constantly clarified and revised, to take into account the progress accomplished by you and your colleagues.*

An *Ippon* for throwing is only given to a throw that makes *uke* "fly" very fast and fall flat onto his back.

When all conditions aren't met but a standing attack produces results, you may be given a partial score which, however, does not put an end to the fight.

◆ *Waza-ari*, if a player almost deserves *ippon*, but one of the conditions was unsatisfactory, such as lack of speed

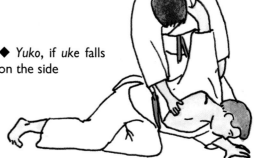

◆ *Yuko*, if *uke* falls on the side

◆ *Koka*, if *uke* lands on his thigh or buttocks and his back is not against the ground

An *ippon* through *osaekomi* is usually given only for 30 seconds of continuous hold. A *waza-ari* may be called if the hold lasts between 25 and 29 seconds; *yuko*, between 20 and 24 seconds; and *koka*, between 15 and 19 seconds.

*These are the numeric values of the partial scores which help in deciding who is the winner.*

| Ippon = 10 points | Waza-ari = 7 points | Yuko = 5 points | Koka = 3 points |

**Here are the penalties, biggest to smallest (*hansoku-make, keikoku, chui, shido*), and corresponding value in "positive points" awarded for valid attacks.**

| Penalties | | Value (positive points) | Equal to partners |
|---|---|---|---|
| Hansoku-make | ➤ disqualification (opponent declared winner) | 10 points | Ippon |
| Keikoku | ➤ severe warning | 7 points | Waza-ari |
| Chui | ➤ warning | 5 points | Yuko |
| Shido | ➤ remark | 3 points | Koka |

*The referee may also "free" warn a fighter for an action or behavior that may cause a sanction if repeated.*

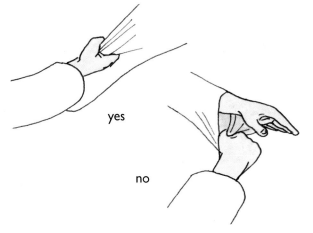

To show clearly that the spirit of judo is to win through attack, and not by simply preventing a partner's attacks, a referee gives a penalty to anyone who attempts nothing. The penalty may increase should that player still not attack. It may even result in a player losing the fight (*hansoku-make*).

A player may also be penalized for actions that are prohibited by the rules of combat:

◆ leaving the *tatami* voluntarily

◆ gripping the partner in an illegal way (by the inside of the sleeve, for example)

yes

no

During a fight, watch the scoreboard. At each recess you can confirm your score.

◆ behaving dangerously or in a cruel manner (deliberately hitting with fists, feet, head or knees

# GENERAL IMPROVEMENT

## PHASE TWO

### *Orange, Orange/Green and Green Belts*
# *Techniques and Tactics*

You are starting to have a basic understanding of judo,
although there's still much to discover.
You can now concentrate on developing everything you have learned.

## *Standing Combat : Nagewaza*

*You have examined all the combination moves done with your partner, no matter which of you initiates the attack. You know which direction is preferable as an attack for each of those movements. You are constantly working to improve your favorite attacks, using* uchikomi *and others.*

**Here are some new throwing techniques
for you to learn**...

## 1. Uchimata

You have certainly seen and admired this technique, performed by more advanced judoka. In its basic form this is a foot technique (*ashiwaza*). But you can also execute it with a hip movement (*koshiwaza*).

*Uchimata* is an impressive technique with many variations. It consists of sweeping the inside of the opponent's thigh, who turns as if he were, badly mounted on a horse, on a slanting ramp.

## 2. Tsurikomi-goshi

Like an *ogoshi*, it is a hip throw, but instead of pushing *uke* on the upper back with your right hand, you pull him from the front (still not letting go off his lapel).

The difficulty is in positioning your arm well, with the elbow "out" and not "inside" as in *morote-seoinage*.

For a big change: you can, with your guard on your right side, apply *tsurikomi-goshi* on the left by pushing your partner's elbow up, with your arm "supporting" his, or by pushing his arm upward and then pulling it down.

*Sode-tsurikomi-goshi*

## 3. Taniotoshi

This is a first *sutemiwaza* (sacrifice technique) that you are learning. The weight of your body, dropped voluntarily, forces your opponent to fall with you.

This may reveal a new tactical idea for you: you attack him when he starts positioning himself for attack. This is a *sen-no-sen* (attack within the other's attack).

Here are two other *sutemi* for your personal program, especially the one you dreamed of since you first received your white belt: *tomoenage*.

To accomplish it, you have to slide under *uke*, taking care to put your foot into your partner's stomach before your back touches the ground.

And, for the safety of both of you, do *not* pull him in toward you with your hands. Instead, try to bring him down far behind your head.

You will apply *yoko-tomoe*. At this point, he will be too bent for you to pass below him from the front.

# *Tactical Principles*

## 1. Counter-attack after blocking

You know how to block your opponent's attack in *jigotai*, by keeping your body very straight, your legs bent, and *hara* (stomach) hardened. Here is an opportunity to block him: you lift him with an action of legs, pushing with your stomach. This is *ushiro-goshi*.

**Example 1**

**Example 2** Other ways to counter him will appear after you block him:

*Osotogari*

◆ You have learned *ushiro-goshi*, from a block in *jigotai*, and this allows you to "pass below" and then behind him.

◆ You can also block his attack by placing a support, "as a prop," in the direction in which he wants to throw you.

◆ The strong support may become a pivot to be used to throw him.

Countered by *osotogari*

## 2. The idea of confusion

Another new concept in this section: the idea of introducing confusion. You already know how to change an attack after a sidestep or after *uke*'s block. Since you can sense his reactions more quickly, you now have an opportunity to gain some time. You won't simply launch one attack to be followed by another, but prepare to mount an attack that could continue in two different directions. As soon as you notice his defense going in one direction, you can finish your attack in another direction.

# *Standing/Ground Link*

You know standing partial scoring very well and realize that your opponent will always try to "give" you the minimum number of points possible. He will also avoid the *ippon* that would end the fight. Therefore, instead of landing on his back he will try to salvage his falls by instead landing on his side, flat on his stomach, on hands and knees or on his buttocks. You would do the same in his place.

*on the side*

*flat on the stomach*

*on the buttocks*

*on hands and knees*

But what you have scored here is not sufficient. You have to obtain your *ippon*. So, you will follow up on the ground right away, turn him on his back and do *osaekomi*.

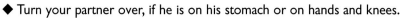

# Ground Combat : Newaza

*In this area of combat, your repertoire becomes even richer.*

## In an upper position, you have already learned to:

◆ Turn your partner over, if he is on his stomach or on hands and knees.

*Kuzure-yoko-shiho-gatame*

*Tate-shiho-gatame*

◆ Get rid of his legs, if he places them between you and himself.

*Yoko-shiho-gatame*

◆ Free your leg, when your partner holds it in between his own.

*Tate-shiho-gatame*

For these three situations you have new solutions and you are now better equipped to surprise your opponent or adapt to his defense system.

**But, in the same three situations, you may find yourself in the lower position.**

Your first concern then is to steal back the initiative, to attack in order to win…
so, you do not stay below.

◆ If being attacked while on your stomach or hands and knees, you need to turn your partner over or at least face him and grasp him with your legs.

◆ Once you have hold of him with your legs, you have to swing him into the most convenient direction for your position, to enable you to conclude with *osaekomi*.

*Kata-gatame*

◆ When you control one of his legs, quickly try to turn him over and hold him before he can "catch" your leg first.

You are studying *kata-gatame*, a method of control by overpowering, not by brutality.

All these tactics link your judo techniques more and more. If your attack or defense attempts fail, or succeed only partially, you can now immediately link to other attempts and adapt to a new situation. When you successfully take an opponent in *osaekomi*, you know how to neutralize attempts to escape, not by freezing in position but by switching to a different support, modifying your grips and using your knee, elbow or head as a "block." Now you feel more comfortable in a lower position, so that when your opponent puts you on your back, you can control him with your legs and turn him over more easily.

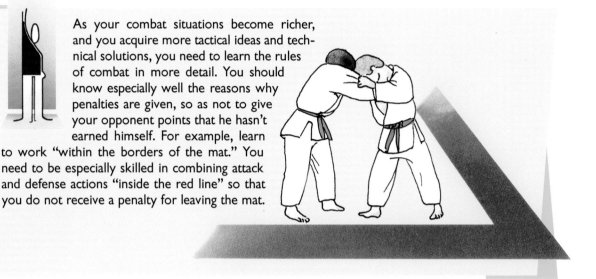

As your combat situations become richer, and you acquire more tactical ideas and technical solutions, you need to learn the rules of combat in more detail. You should know especially well the reasons why penalties are given, so as not to give your opponent points that he hasn't earned himself. For example, learn to work "within the borders of the mat." You need to be especially skilled in combining attack and defense actions "inside the red line" so that you do not receive a penalty for leaving the mat.

You have completed the final stage before the so-called "dark belts," those that directly prepare you for the black belt that marks the judo specialist. Your technical knowledge has been enriched. It will, in fact, continue to grow because the practice of judo has an almost unlimited variety of movements. But you can see that behind the variety lie a small number of fundamental principles that always apply, in various ways and under different forms.

You have grown, matured, become more logical and rational. Now you can tackle more difficult techniques …and succeed.

# Personal Improvement

## a general and an individual program

**Y**ou are poised now to enter the court of the great. For each of the two belts—blue and brown—you will find both a general program, intended for all judoka, and a personal program that you can develop and practice with your trainer.

*As you continue to learn, you develop your judo.
This is a sport that has many discoveries in store for you.
It is as if it were a rich treasure chest, through which you
could rummage all your life and always find new things.
You will know yourself better, your strong and your
weak points, and your preferences.
It is not so easy, if you are young. At such an age, everything
changes fast: your size, weight, strength and your ideas.
Your new program takes all this into account.*

# Blue Belt

## General Program

## Nagewaza

*Below are 5 new throws, all of them forward, but coming from different groups:*

### 1. *Koshiwaza* (hip throw): *hane-goshi*

*Uke* is heaved up, like a full trash bag into a dump truck.

## 2. *Tewaza* (hand throw): *kata-guruma*

*Uke* rolls across *tori*'s shoulders.

## 3. Three *sutemiwaza* (sacrifices)

◆ A *ma-sutemi: sumi-gaeshi*…

*Tori* pulls on a leg with a hook move to bring *uke*'s thighs forward. It's necessary to supply hand support, so that *uke* doesn't collapse on *tori* (valid for *tomoenage*).

◆ and two *yoko-sutemi*: *yoko-guruma* and *soto-makikomi*

For *yoko-guruma*, *tori* has the same attitude and performs the same action as in *taniotoshi*. But here *uke* is slung forward.

For *soto-makikomi*, the basic idea is *koshi-guruma*, plus the power of *sutemi* (*tori*'s body is thrown). Do not aim in front of you, but to the side. Note: *Tori* lands on the side of his thigh (beside *uke*).

# *Newaza*

*N*ow you have enough self-control, psychological maturity
and technical competence to tackle the surrender techniques:
shimewaza *(chokes) and* kansetsuwaza *(arm-locks).*

## Here is your program:

## 1. Three front choke holds

All three are "crossed" (the left hand takes the right side, and the right hand the left):

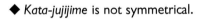
◆ *Kata-jujijime* is not symmetrical.

◆ *Nami-jujijime* and...                    ◆ *gyaku-jujijime* are symmetrical.

## 2. Three rear choke holds

◆ *Hadakajime*

Be careful to retain contact everywhere and to pull *uke*'s head with the shoulder.

◆ *Okurierijime*

Your second hand pulls on the collar to ensure contact everywhere and provokes a rear right-side imbalance.

◆ *Katahajime*

*Uke*, threatened by *okurierijime*, tries to seize *tori*'s head. *Tori* first controls the shoulder, then destabilizes *uke* from the rear-left side.

# 3. Leg choke: *sankakujime*

You've known how to do the "triangle" (padlock) since you were a white belt. This time, however, not only do you seize *uke*'s leg, but his neck and an arm as well.

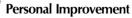

## 4. Locks: *kansetsuwaza*

In judo, the locks (which threaten dislocation of articulation) apply only to the elbow.

◆ *Juji-gatame*

For control of the shoulder, one leg drives into the armpit, the second leg "brings" the gluteus onto the heel.

◆ *Udegarami*

*Uke*'s hand is bent and not tight like in *juji-gatame*.

All locked up and under perfect control, no harm comes to *uke*. The action is decisive and the range of movement is small if the lock is done well (little strength is necessary).

**Attention:**
You must stop immediately when *uke* taps several times to indicate surrender.

The most important principle in surrender technique is always to establish beforehand every contact necessary to lock the position and to control *uke*, and *only then* apply the final action.

It is necessary to do this for your partner's security: the golden rule is always essential. It must be done also to be certain of receiving an *ippon*.

# *Shimewaza, Kansetsuwaza and Jujitsu*

In jujitsu (the precursor of judo) there was no question of winning matches, but combat to the death. The nobles in feudal Japan, continually at war, had to practice constantly to perfect their martial arts. Consequently, many jujitsu schools developed.

The *bijin* (warrior), particularly, could win a fight even without arms, by striking with the hands, feet, elbows, etc. (*atemiwaza*). He could also render his opponent powerless by tying him up, to earn a ransom (*hojojitsu*). He could disable an opponent by dislocating a shoulder, elbow or knee (*kansetsuwaza*). He could kill him or render him unconscious by strangling (*shimewaza*).

When Dr. Jigoro Kano created judo, he was able to conserve the traditions of this warrior past, while eliminating danger and brutality, and preserve its educational side (refined technique and self-control). *Shimewaza* and *kansetsuwaza* (only to the elbow) bear witness to this approach: they were created to conquer an opponent, not by doing him harm, but by demonstrating control over him. This is why, in judo competition, a referee may call *ippon* when he decides that a *shimewaza* or *kansetsuwaza* has gained sufficient control, even if the "locked" player hasn't yet surrendered.

In judo you can also find *atemiwaza*, as well as utilization of arms: *tanto* (dagger), *bo* (stick) and *katana* (sword). But they serve only to point up defense without arms, and are used in *katas* (pre-organized demonstration forms).

Some schools, concerned about preserving judo's "martial art" aspect, which is now a great international sport, have developed and organized jujitsu practice. Their *judoka* are taught elements of jujitsu as part of their judo program, starting from the green belt. *Judoka* entering through jujitsu may have to spend extra time studying judo techniques—in particular, throws.

*The handling of traditional weapons can pose a serious threat to the unprepared. Strength and balance must be mastered first, so beginners and young players should not attempt it.*

# *Katas*

Katas *are set forms of the martial arts. They exist not only in judo, but also in karate and in kung fu, where they are called "taos," which means "forms"—like the Japanese word.*

These demonstrations, in which everything is standardized—ceremonial, form and succession of attack and defense—represent a true "conservation" of the martial art to which they belong.

*Katas* allow us, for a time, to live judo the way the masters did. These forms were created by experts of the art, considered the best in their time, often with the help of the founder of the school—for many *judoka* that is Dr. Jigoro Kano. Therefore, *katas* are completely different than what is seen in many drawings, photographs or movies.

*Katas* are not boring exercises, if you don't look at them as simplistic lessons to repeat. Just as artists like to reproduce paintings of the masters—not simply "copy" them but feel the movements directly with their hands, eyes and brain, and modeling their master in reproducing the exact forms and colors—*judoka* like to perform *katas* with maximal submission to the idea hidden there, and at the same time with maximum spontaneity and expression of the *judoka*'s own personality. Moreover, if possible this should be done in direct unity with a partner who has the same sensitivity. But this is very difficult and rare, as are all precious things.

# Forms of Throwing: Nagenokata

*Nagenokata consists of five series, of three techniques each, that are performed to the right and to the left.*

Each series illustrates a single throw category:

**Series 1: Tewaza**
hand techniques (arms, shoulders)
1. Ukiotoshi
2. Ipponseoinage
3. Kataguruma

**Series 2: Koshiwaza**
hip techniques
1. Ukigoshi
2. Haraigoshi
3. Tsurikomigoshi

**Series 3: Ashiwaza**
leg techniques
1. Okuriashibarai
2. Sasaetsurikomiashi
3. Uchimata

**Series 4: Masutemiwaza**
"straight-on" sacrifice techniques
1. Tomoenage
2. Uranage
3. Sumigaeshi

**Series 5: Yokosutemiwaza**
sacrifice techniques "from the side"
1. Yokogake
2. Yokoguruma
3. Ukiwaza

**At the testing for first *dan* (grade) you present only the first three series.**

The general scenario is as follows:

◆ *Uke* attacks *tori*, either by moving closer to him or by throwing a punch at him

◆ *Tori* dodges the attack and destabilizes *uke*

◆ *Tori* throws *uke*

Many techniques are executed in three steps: dodging, unbalancing and throwing. These three stages, done in actual combat in a single step, are separated here in order for the judges to see them clearly and to evaluate the two partners' proficiency.

The fact that certain of *uke*'s attacks take on the form of punches reveals that judo came from jujitsu.

In practicing *nagenokata,* you must be able to present it with "sincerity." This means that, while performing the pre-planned techniques in the specified order and form, the *uke* has to really attack and not simply arrange to take a fall, and the *tori* has to throw with strength and conviction.

# Personal Program

*Analysis of your judo attacks and defense moves will allow you to improve even more.*

To be efficient, the response to each change must be immediate. This ability to launch the right technique at the appropriate moment characterizes the art of the *judoka*. It requires having a personal, "constructed" judo that allows you to attack in different directions, with different linking techniques.

### You have to be able to, at the same time:

◆ Exploit each opportunity offered by your partner

◆ Create other opportunities by moving, tricks and provoking him to react

Here are two examples for your *tokuiwaza* (favorite technique):

◆ *Osotogari* to the right, which can lead to *harai-goshi* or *o-uchigari*.

◆ *O-uchigari* to the right (which can lead to *harai-goshi*)

Osotogari

Harai-goshi

O-uchigari

*The attack system is rather complete (three directions), but all the attacks are performed with the help of the right leg.*

You can evaluate your abilities by using a small diagram, such as the one at right. Draw it on two cards, one for attack and one for defense. Indicate losses or gains—*koka*, *yuko*, *waza-ari* and *ippon*—by marking the section where you obtained them.

Ask a friend to keep the cards, and you, in turn, can fill out his. Fill out an "attack" and a "defense" card each time you participate in a competition, either official or casual. It will allow you to direct efforts to strengthening weak points. "Attack" cards that are filled out three months apart will reveal any changes in efficiency.

**Example of scorekeeping:**

*Koka* for *ko-uchigari*
*Yuko* for *o-uchigari*
*Waza-ari* for *harai-goshi*

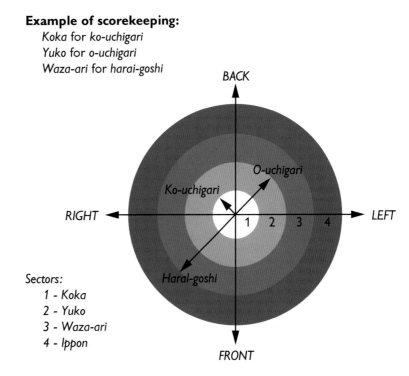

*Sectors:*
1 - *Koka*
2 - *Yuko*
3 - *Waza-ari*
4 - *Ippon*

**All this is the beginning of your personalized combat system, which you will be improving bit by bit: making it stronger, more logical and more complete.**

You have chosen your favorite attacks (*tokuiwaza*) for *randori*, or refereed fights, long ago. Your regular partners know them, too, and know what you will likely try when you are their opponent. It's possible that, over time, one or more of these *tokuiwaza* may change, or be added. A newly learned throw may appeal to you because it "feels" right or because a champion you admire uses it. You've seen it work, so you adopt it. On ground technique, you're looking for one or two *osaekomi* you can do well.

◆ **Stronger**
  • by working a lot on your best movements in *uchikomi*, *nagekomi* and *randori*

◆ **More logical**
  • by adapting your *kumikata* and movements to your *tokuiwaza*
  • by improving your defense from the counter-attacks that may be launched by your opponent after your attacks

  • by researching the most favorable and certain links to your preferred *osaekomi*

◆ **More complete**
  • by choosing and working on preparatory attacks that may provoke the opponent to make a step or assume a position that will allow you to use your *tokuiwaza*
  • by working on other attacks to which you can transfer if the partner dodges your *tokuiwaza*

Another important aspect of your combat system to work on…

# First Moves: Confrontation

This occurs in the beginning after *hajime*, during the fight, and after *matte* and a new *hajime*. You have to think of a way to approach your opponent, to seize his *judogi* rapidly and strongly, in a position favorable for an immediate attack.

*ai-hammi*

Which hand do you prefer to use first? Where will you grab? Will it be useful as is or will you need to watch for a chance to improve your grip?

Is the grab just a trick, or intermediate to an action by your other, stronger hand? How will you switch to it?

How can you seize better, and at the same time prevent the other from seizing?

*gyaku-hammi*

*at the top*

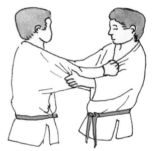

*at the bottom*

*bring closer to seize*

*push to seize*

These are the questions to which you have to find answers, *your* own answers. In order to do this, you need to devote your time and attentions and come up with exercises to do with a partner whom you can ask to "bother" you in such a way that you can work up appropriate responses.

All these patient and precise efforts also have to take into account the changes that you will normally bring to your system, either because you have discovered a new strong movement or because, the next time you fight, you want to surprise opponents who know your combat moves a little too well.

# *Brown Belt*

## General Program

## *Nagewaza*

*Here are some new, higher-level techniques:*

### A new counter by lifting: *utsuri-goshi*

### Two throws seizing by the legs: *morote-gari* and…

## *kuchiki-daoshi*

With these two throws, pay attention to the regulations of the specific fight. If you are not alert, not only won't you score points with these throws, but using one may cost you a penalty.

Although junior fighters are prohibited from executing these throws, they need to be studied in order to earn advancement to the category of young athlete.

**You have already learned 38 *nagewaza* techniques. Each of them, in its particular form, uses and illustrates a certain number of basic ideas that you can now recognize and understand.**

◆ Reaping (*gari*), sweep (*harai, barai*), hook (*gake sasae*) of *uke*'s support
◆ Unbalance, turn over, or twist *uke*'s body
◆ Duck under him, place your opponent in space, cause *uke* to trip
◆ "Sacrificing" (*sutemi*), using the weight of your falling body to pull *uke* down
◆ Researching angles and body contacts with *uke* that will favor a throw

**By keeping these basic ideas in mind, you can even improve the performance of your least familiar throws.**

# Newaza

*Adding to the two locks that you already know, here are four more that you can use in different positions:*

## 1. Ude-gatame
**(control by the arm)**

## 2. Waki-gatame
**(control by the armpit)**

# 3. Ashi-gatame (control by the feet)

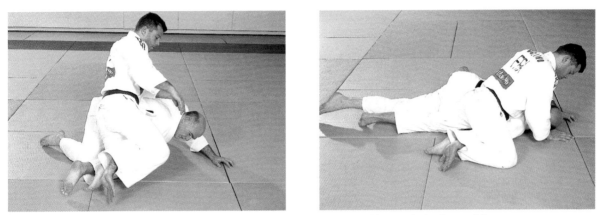

You meet again an old acquaintance, the control by *sankaku* (triangle).

## To score an *ippon* on the ground, you can now use:

◆ 6 basic *osaekomi* positions with numerous variations

◆ 6 forms of locks, applicable in many positions

◆ 7 choke techniques, from front or rear

And in order to make these decisive holds, you know many turns and reversals that bring the action to the ground from standing combat.

If you have done your work well, you will be able to pass the technical tests of *nagewaza* and *newaza* should you decide to obtain your first *dan* through technical expression.

### As with *nagewaza*, you have basic ideas:

◆ Reap, sweep, block a support, but on the ground it's not only the legs that play a role.

◆ Create a rotation that pulls your partner with you; or, opposite, prevents him from turning.

◆ Concentrate many forces on one point. For example, in *juji-gatame*, all four of your limbs oppose one of his arms.

◆ Play in an aligned or crossed position.

◆ Place "corners" (elbow, knee and head) on your partner.

◆ Find spaces to change your angle or interpose your limb for defense.

# Personal Program
## Building on Your Standing Combat

## *Nagewaza*

### Some issues to work on in your *kumikata*

◆ You're left-handed, he's right-handed: how do you counter his *kumikata* while securing yours?

◆ Have you practiced your "firsthand" attacks, to throw at first grip?

◆ Can you neutralize the attack or seize the opponent's strong hand to launch an offensive?

# Improving your throws

◆ Are your "preparatory" attacks strong enough to score at least a *koka*? Or are they able to "disturb" your opponent and possibly force him to make a hazardous move, distort his posture or change hand, leaving him only one type of grip?

◆ Do you have instant links, in the face of popular defensive moves, that trigger your favorite attack?

◆ Have you thoroughly studied the ground moves that come at the end of your standing attacks or your counters to your partner's attacks?

*Okurierijime*

# Newaza

### Improving your ground mobility

◆ Seize all the opportunities to change angle, link or control; during the ground *randori* try to vary your moves as much as possible. Don't just systematically use your *tokuiwaza*.

◆ Concentrate practice on working from the inferior position: your knowledge of *shimewaza* and *kansetsuwaza* will open many chances to win from the ground position—even if staying there.

## Completing your personal system

◆ Can you integrate *shimewaza* or *kansetsuwaza* as responses to attempts of release from *osaekomi*?

◆ or as threats that will help you to free yourself?

◆ or, finally, as a threat that leads to an *ippon*, or a way of turning over your opponent when he takes refuge in stomach defense?

# Physical Conditioning

*T*o make further progress in judo and to build a strong physique, you have much to do in and out of the dojo:

◆ Reinforce your "engine"—your heart and lungs—by being active outdoors. Efforts should not be very intense, but sustained and frequent. Jogging or biking are good activities for this purpose.

◆ Facilitate your growth by maintaining good hygiene and a regular and balanced diet. In addition, maintain good sleep habits: sleep enough and well (calm, good air circulation).

◆ Become tougher by gradually increasing the rhythm, duration and repetition of your judo or other exercises, and don't forget to relax and stretch after each activity.

◆ Gain better efficiency and avoid "small accidents" (cramps, strains or sprains) by seriously warming up before each training session and competition, by respecting the return to calm after important activities and by remembering to rehydrate yourself.

# *How to better prepare for combat*

**1. Start the machine:** light but rather lengthy activities (5 to 10 minutes)

**2. Warm up the motor:** average activities, until you feel the heat

**3. Verify direction and breaks:** stretches, relaxing, sharp movements (not maximal strength)

**4. Prepare the route:** study, *uchikomi*, *yaku-soku-geiko* on the ground…

Your trainer will give you helpful advice on all these points, but you are the person most responsible. Watch your pulse and weight. Adapt your warm-up to the session that will follow.

# How to monitor your heart

◆ *Take your pulse*

Contact must be gentle, so as not to interrupt circulation.

◆ *Monitor your pulse*

- Take your waking pulse without getting up or moving too much (use a watch from your night stand).

- Take your resting pulse during the day, far from any activity (and not after a big meal).

- Take your activity pulse immediately after the activity, for 15 seconds, and multiply it by 4 to get the beats per minute.

- Take your recovery pulse for the next 15 seconds; then after 1 minute, 2 minutes and again 3 minutes after the activity.

**Some guidelines:**

The waking pulse is slower than the resting pulse.
The resting pulse is slower than the activity pulse.
The rhythm of the activity pulse, during long and fairly intense work, should not exceed 140–150 beats per minute. Your trainer should examine your specific case.
The rhythm of the recovery pulse should slow gradually 1, 2 or 3 minutes after the activity.

Plan for physical activities, even during vacations.

With a little bit of good luck, and some thoughtful organization of your personal life, you can expect to remain in excellent health as long as you live ...and to continue practicing judo for a long time. In any case, this is what we wish for you.

## *First Dan*
# *The Black Belt*

*At the end of your long initial period of training
comes your presentation for first dan.
At last, the grand moment has arrived!*

You have done your best to become capable of acquitting yourself honorably throughout the tests. You have learned patience. You have trained courageously and relentlessly to prepare yourself. You have struggled to bring credit to your trainer, your club and to judo.

During your years of work, successive grades have accompanied your progress. Now your trainer believes that you can achieve your black belt. He is confident enough to let others evaluate you.

## To obtain a first-degree black belt

Starting from the young athlete category, the *judoka* who have received
the first *kyu* (brown belt) over a year ago and who are authorized
by their trainer to pass the test may apply.

**Schools generally have two ways of obtaining a black belt, such as:**

◆ **competition** (3 tests)

First *dan* may be awarded to candidates who have scored a cumulative 100 points in several competitions, or 44 points at one time during an official competition or *shodan-shiken* (competition for the grades). Testing is completed by the presentation of *nagenokata* (first three series), and by apprenticeship as a sport commissioner, or organizer of competitions.

◆ **technical expression** (7 C.U.)

First *dan* may be awarded to candidates completing 7 required Course Units of instruction during organized regional-level examinations.

C.U. 1: experience as a sport commissioner
C.U. 2: standing technique (*nagewaza*)
C.U. 3: ground technique (*newaza*) (jujitsu)
C.U. 4: training methods
C.U. 5: *katas*
C.U. 6: defense techniques (jujitsu)
C.U. 7: combat

**The fact that you are presenting yourself for first *dan* opens up
new horizons for you in judo: you need to understand
how the two ways, competition and technical expression,
determine the same combined value of *shin-ghi-tai* through different means.**

# *Shin-ghi-tai*

### The mind: *shin*

You first learned respect for ceremony, to become attentive, patient, courageous.

Now you know courtesy, even in small details, for your partner and for judo, makes you more appreciated and stronger.

You now can apply great force in combat and, when your hear "*soremade*," can return immediately to absolute calm. Experience has taught that each effort has payback, if not immediate or in the way expected.

You have developed your mental fortitude, and you use your will in a good direction. This is one of three components of the grade.

### The technique: *ghi*

You have studied for many hours, repeating and exploring the subtleties of a great number of complex attack and defense actions. With the help of your trainer, you gradually learned the underlying ideas, or "principles."

Now you know the rules of combat and can discover the subtleties of its applications. You can make tactical calculations that did not even enter your mind when you were a white belt.

You have developed your knowledge and your technical repertoire, acquired the know-how and have become more competent. This is the second component of the grade.

### The fighter's worth: *tai*

All the hours of sweating, hard breathing, training stiffness
have forged a powerful body that responds skillfully and without
delay. It shows in the quality of your fights, whether won or lost—the best players congratulate you and enjoy working with you, and the less advanced have confidence in you. You have developed the qualities of a fighter. This is the third component of the grade.

You are starting to suspect that there is no limit to progress in judo, but also that no person
is perfect in all respects—yet everyone has his merits and his value.
Now you must develop your own personal judo program in more depth. It is time to determine
what you want to give judo and what you want from judo in return. This special judo "project"
may become even more important to you in the future. Who knows?—it may become
the main thing in your life, the man or woman you want to be.

# *Competition*

**long-awaited time of testing**

Competition is an essential stage in the development of your judo. By using the mental and physical resources you have built up, you can now prove your know-how, test yourself against opponents and continue to increase your progress. Victory is beautiful and defeats should always be constructive.

You can practice judo all your life, but you can participate in competitions for only a few years. Take advantage of this! Competing puts all of your abilities to the test.

You must also have a sound knowledge of the rules of judo combat.

# *Competition Procedures*

**1.** The two scheduled fighters approach from each side of the combat area, according to their color (white, red), make a greeting upon entering the *tatami* and position themselves on the places indicated.

**2.** They greet each other and wait.

**3.** When the referee calls out "*hajime*," the fighters advance on each other to begin the combat.

**4.** If the referee should announce "*matte*," the fighters release each other, immediately separate and return to their places, according to color.

**5.** If the referee announces "*ippon*" or "*sore-made*," the fighters return to their places to greet each other and wait for the announced result of the match.

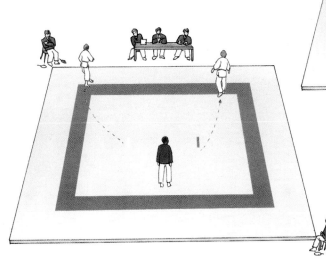

**6.** When the result is announced, the fighters leave the mat the same way they entered, remembering to make another greeting at the edge of the *tatami*.

# Combat Zones

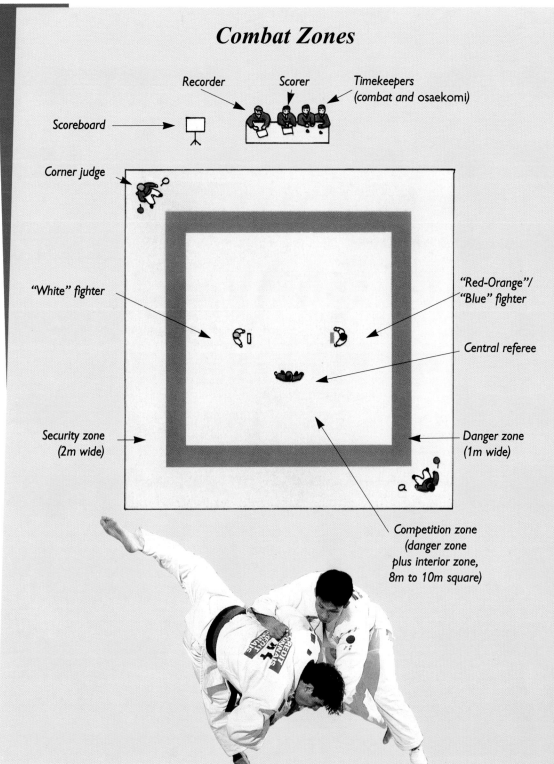

Recorder

Scorer

Timekeepers
(combat and osaekomi)

Scoreboard

Corner judge

"White" fighter

"Red-Orange"/
"Blue" fighter

Central referee

Security zone
(2m wide)

Danger zone
(1m wide)

Competition zone
(danger zone
plus interior zone,
8m to 10m square)

# *Forms of Competition*

# Pool

## Take, for example, a pool of 3 fighters:

It is agreed that the one who does not fight acts as referee. After three fights, each player will have fought with the two others…and refereed once. The winner is the one with more victories. With an equal number of victories, the one who has more points wins. With an equal number of victories and points, the winner of a fight between the two fighters is declared winner of the tournament.

*A loss by* ippon *against B*

*C won by* waza-ari *against B*

*B MEETS C, A IS REFEREE*
*A MEETS C, B IS REFEREE*
*A MEETS B, C IS REFEREE*

|   | A | B | C | Total | Rank |
|---|---|---|---|-------|------|
| A |   | 0 | 0 | 0 | 3rd |
| B | 10 |   | 0 | 10 | 2nd |
| C | 5 | 7 |   | 12 | 1st |

## Another example, a pool of 5 fighters:

|   | 1 | 2 | 3 | 4 | 5 |
|---|---|---|---|---|---|
| 1 |   |   |   |   |   |
| 2 |   |   |   |   |   |
| 3 |   |   |   |   |   |
| 4 |   |   |   |   |   |
| 5 |   |   |   |   |   |

The results are written in the light-colored squares.

No fighter participates in two competitions in a row if the 10 matches are organized as follows:
1-2, 3-4, 1-5, 2-3, 4-5, 1-3, 2-4, 3-5, 1-4, 2-5

# Knockout

The fighters are allocated an order of passage: No. 1, 2, 3, etc. The matches follow this order each time the winner qualifies for the next combat. In case of a tie, both opponents are eliminated.

The fighter who wins more matches (or, in case of an equal number, more points) wins the knockout competition.

**Example: 1 2 3 4 5 6 7 8**

1 against 2: 1 winner
1 against 3: 3 winner
3 against 4: 3 winner
3 against 5: 3 winner

3 against 6: 6 winner
6 against 7: 7 winner
7 against 8: 7 winner
7 against 1: 1 winner

No. 3 wins this line (3 victories) against No. 7 (2 victories).

# Lineup Board

The names of the fighters are listed at the left on a lineup board. Each competes with another fighter, as shown by the arrows. After each round of fights, the winners go on to compete in the order indicated on the board. The finals (the last round), in which only two fighters are left, determine the winner of the competition.

If there is an uneven number of registered fighters to compete (not 8, 16, 32, 64, etc.), the number is "evened out" through a preliminary fight for which the fighters are drawn by lot.

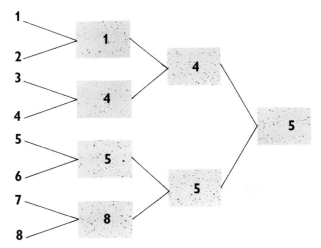

This scoreboard's winner is fighter number 5. Fighters numbered 6, 8 and 4 (all defeated by 5) are allowed to qualify and continue the competition for third place.

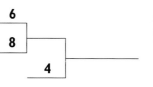

# Referee's Hand Signals

Referees use a language of signals that can be understood by everyone.

*hajime*

*matte*

*ippon*

*osaokomi*

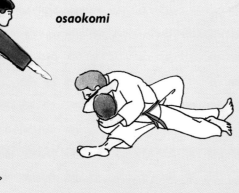

*toketa*

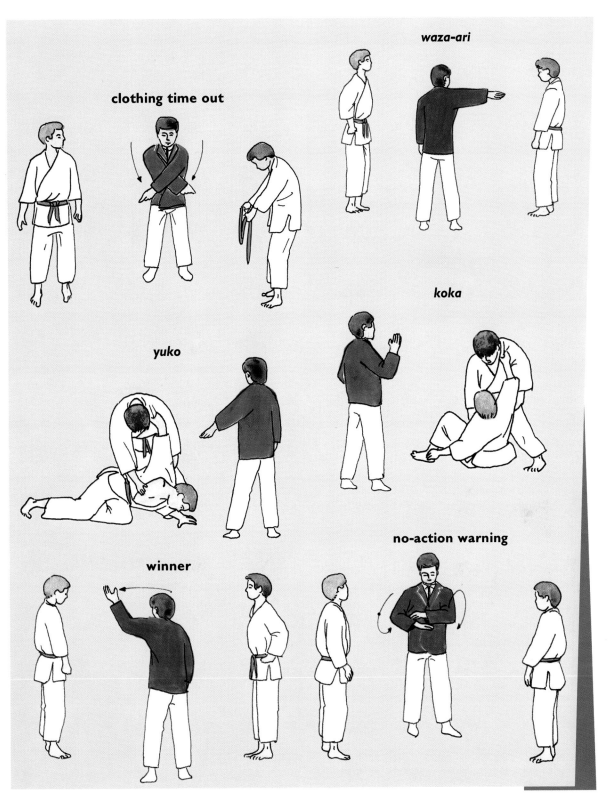

waza-ari

clothing time out

koka

yuko

no-action warning

winner

# Vocabulary

From judo's founder, Dr. Jigoro Kano, and the influence of Japanese tradition you can understand why all the words used in judo are from that language. By hearing and using the terms, judoka often end up speaking (if just a little… ) Japanese; you will likely find yourself learning bits of the language almost without noticing.

| | Japanese word | Pronunciation | Translation |
|---|---|---|---|
| **a** | **ashiwaza** | ash-i-wa-za | foot and leg techniques |
| | **ayumi-ashi** | ajoo-mi-ash-i | normal walking |
| **c** | **chui** | chew-i | penalty |
| **d** | **dan** | dan | grade |
| | **de-ashi-barai** | day-ash-i-barai | advancing foot sweep |
| | **dojo** | doh-joh | a place where Japanese martial arts are studied and practiced |
| **e** | **eri-seoinage** | eh-ri-seh-oh-ee-nah-geh | shoulder throw (by collar) |
| **g** | **gachi** | gah-chi | winner |
| | **ghi** | ghih | the technique (competence) |
| | **gyaku-jujijime** | gee-ya-kuh-joo-ji-ji-meh | reverse choke, hands "inside out" (palms looking up) |
| **h** | **hadakajime** | ha-da-ka-ji-may | "bare" choke (without cloth) |
| | **hajime** | ha-ji-may | begin |
| | **hanegoshi** | ha-neh-goh-shi | spring hip throw "in attack" |
| | **hansoku-make** | shihan-soh-kuh-mah-kay | disqualification |
| | **hara-gatame** | ha-ra-ga-tah-may | lock "by the stomach" |
| | **haraigoshi** | ha-ra-i-goh-shi | "sweeping" hip throw |
| | **hidari** | hi-da-ri | left, to the left |
| | **hikiwake** | hi-ki-wah-kay | draw |
| | **hizaguruma** | hi-za-guh-roo-mah | knee wheel |
| | **hon-gesa-gatame** | hon-geh-sah-ga-tah-may | basic "scarf" hold |
| **i** | **ippon** | i-pon | one point (in a fight) |
| | **ippon-seoinage** | i-pon-seh-oh-i-nah-geh | shoulder throw by one side |
| **j** | **jigotai** | jih-goh-tah-i | low defensive attitude/posture |
| | **judo** | joo-doh | the way of gentleness |
| | **judogi** | joo-doh-gi | clothing worn for judo |
| | **juji-gatame** | joo-ji-gah-tah-may | straight armlock |
| | **jujitsu** | joo-jit-soo | technique and art of gentleness |
| **k** | **kami-shiho-gatame** | ka-mi-shi-ho-gah-tah-may | "upper" lock |
| | **kakari-geiko** | ka-ka-ri-gay-koh | "only one attack" training |
| | **kansetsuwaza** | kan-set-soo-wa-za | locking techniques (locks) |

| | | | |
|---|---|---|---|
| | kata | ka-ta | shoulder, and also "form" |
| | kata-guruma | ka-ta-guh-roo-mah | shoulder wheel |
| | kata-jujijime | ka-ta-joo-ji-ji-may | cross choke with a hand |
| | keikoku | keh-ee-koh-koo | severe penalty |
| | kesa-gatame | keh-sah-gah-tah-may | "scarf" lock |
| | koka | koh-ka | small advantage |
| | kosotogake | koh-so-to-gah-kay | outer "minor" leg hook |
| | koshiguruma | koh-shi-guh-ruu-mah | hip wheel |
| | koshiwaza | koh-shi-wah-zah | hip techniques |
| | ko-uchigari | koh-uh-chi-gah-ri | minor inner reaping |
| | kumikata | kuh-mi-ka-ta | gripping (grasping the cloth) |
| | kuzure-gesa-gatame | kuh-zuh-reh-ge-sa-ga-tah-may | variation of a "scarf" hold |
| **m** | mae-ukemi | mah-e-uh-keh-mi | forward breakfall |
| | makura-gesa-gatame | mah-koo-rah-geh-sa-ga-ta-may | "pillow" hold |
| | matte | mah-teh | stop, let go, keep distance |
| | migi | mi-gi | right, to the right |
| | morote-seoinage | moh-roh-teh-she-oh-ee-nah-ge | shoulder throw with two hands |
| **n** | nagekomi | nah-geh-ko-mi | "wave" of throws |
| | nagenokata | nah-geh-noh-ka-ta | form of throws |
| | nagewaza | nah-geh-wah-za | throwing techniques |
| | nami-jujijime | nah-mi-joo-ji-ji-may | crossed hands choke, "right side out" |
| | newaza | neh-wah-za | ground techniques |
| **o** | obi | oh-bi | belt |
| | ogoshi | oh-goh-shi | major hip throw |
| | oguruma | oh-guh-roo-mah | great wheel (hips) |
| | okuri-ashi-barai | oh-kuh-ri-ash-i-ba-rai | ankle sweep "while pursuing" |
| | okuri-erijime | oh-kuh-ri-eh-ri-ji-may | choke "pursuing the reverse" |
| | osotogari | oh-soh-toh-ga-ri | major outer reaping |
| | osaekomi | oh-sah-eh-koh-mi | holding down on back |
| | o-uchigari | oh-uh-chi-ga-ri | major inner reaping |
| **r** | randori | ran-doh-ri | free-moving practice |
| | rei | reh-i | bow |
| | ritsu-rei | rit-suh-reh-i | standing bow |
| **s** | sankaku | san-kah-ku | three sides (triangle) |
| | sankakujime | san-kah-ku-ji-may | "triangle" choke |
| | sasae-tsurikomi-ashi | sah-sae-tsoo-ri-koh-mi-a-shi | low pull throw over ankle (like fishing cast) |
| | seiza | sei-zah | kneeled position |
| | shiai | shi-ah-i | contest |
| | shido | shi-doh | comment, warning |
| | shimewaza | shi-meh-wa-za | choke techniques |
| | shin | shin | "mind," moral value |
| | shizentai | shi-zen-tah-i | basic standing posture |
| | sode-tsurikomi-goshi | soh-day-tsoo-ri-koh-mi-goh-shi | pull throw by sleeve over hip (like fishing cast) |
| | sogogachi | soh-goh-gah-chi | winner by addition (2 *waza-ari*) |

| | | | |
|---|---|---|---|
| | sonomama | soh-noh-mah-mah | "do not move" |
| | soto-makikomi | soh-toh-mah-ki-koh-mi | outer-winding throw |
| | sukuinage | soo-koo-ee-nah-gay | scooping throw |
| | sumi-gaeshi | soo-mi-ga-eh-shi | corner throw (*sutemi* throw) |
| | sutemiwaza | soo-teh-mi-wa-za | sacrifice techniques |
| **t** | tachiwaza | ta-chi-wa-za | "non-*sutemi*" techniques |
| | tai | tah-i | physical, "body" value |
| | taiotoshi | tah-i-o-tosh-i | collapsing throw of *tori* |
| | taniotoshi | ta-ni-o-tosh-i | valley drop |
| | tatami | ta-tam-i | judo mat (personal, 2m by 1m measure) |
| | tate-shiho-gatame | ta-teh-shi-hoh-ga-tah-may | front hold (mounted) |
| | teguruma | teh-guh-roo-mah | hand wheel |
| | toketa-toketa | toh-ket-ta-toh-ket-ta | "escape from *osaekomi*" |
| | tomoenage | toh-moh-eh-na-geh | circle throw (*sutemi*) |
| | tori | toh-ri | the attacking player |
| | tsugiashi | t-soo-gi-ash-i | a walk where one foot always leads |
| | tsurikomi-goshi | t-soo-ri-koh-mi-goh-shi | lifting, pulling hip throw |
| **u** | uchikomi | uh-chi-koh-mi | "to contact from inside" ("entrances") |
| | uchimata | uh-chi-ma-tah | inner-thigh throw |
| | ude-garami | uh-deh-ga-rah-mi | arm-reversal lock |
| | uke | uh-keh | the attacked player, to whom a technique is applied |
| | ukemiwaza | uh-keh-mi-wa-za | falling technique |
| | ukigoshi | uh-ki-goh-shi | floating hip throw |
| | ukiotoshi | uh-ki-o-toh-shi | floating drop |
| | ukiwaza | uh-ki-wa-za | floating throw (*sutemi*) |
| | uranage | uh-rah-nah-gay | forward *sutemi* throw of *tori* |
| | ushiro-gesa-gatame | uh-shi-roh-geh-sah-ga-tah-may | "scarf" control from behind |
| | ushiro-goshi | uh-shi-roh-goh-shi | hip counter-move from behind |
| | utsuri-goshi | ut-soo-ri-goh-shi | "changed" hip counter |
| **w** | waki-gatame | wa-ki-ga-tah-may | armpit hold |
| | waza | wa-za | technique(s), "takes" |
| | waza-ari | wa-za-a-ri | nearly *ippon* (well-executed technique) |
| | waza-ari-awasete-ippon | wa-za-a-ri-ah-wah-she-teh-ee-pon | another *waza-ari*, for total of *ippon* |
| **y** | yaku-soku-geiko | ya-koo-so-koo-gay-koh | training system (everyone attacks in his turn) |
| | yoko-guruma | yoh-koh-guh-roo-mah | *sutemi* side throw, like wheel |
| | yoshi | yo-shi | start again (after *sonomama*) |
| | yuko | yoo-koh | big effect (bigger than *koka*) |
| **z** | zarei | zah-reh-i | ceremonial bow (kneeling) |
| | zoori | zooh-ri | slippers (so as not to walk barefoot) |

# *Index*

# Index